Chords Th

Know

by Barry Maz

Keep Strumming....

Cover photograph – image copyright Barry Maz 2012

INTRODUCTION

The idea of putting out some chord charts in a book has been nagging at me for some time. At the end of the day, you can find countless chord charts that you can print off all over the web. But I started to speak with some ukulele-playing friends and took their feedback. The suggestion was that a book of ukulele chords, including a book in e-format would be a welcome addition to the series of books put out by Got A Ukulele.

Just a few notes on using the book: The book is split in to four key sections, Standard uke chords for GCEA tuning, Standard uke chords with chord fingerings for the left handed player (now then – you don't see that very often do ya?!), standard Baritone chords (just the basic ones) in DGBE tuning, and a similar Baritone section for left handed players.

Now before you email me, the book doesn't contain EVERY single ukulele chord – that would be cumbersome, and as my books are aimed at the beginner, this book contains all of what I think are the most common chords you will come across. To read the chords, I have used black blobs to represent which fret to hold the particular string at. I have not chosen to give finger placings because they annoy me. A chord can be played any number of ways and with whatever fingers you find comfortable so long as you are holding the chord the right way. Take the C chord for example. It is played with just one finger, on the A string at the third fret. Which finger do you use? Well for me it depends on which chord I am moving to it from, or which chord I am moving to. In all seriousness I have used all my fingers to play the C chord, and that goes for all the other chords too. There are no rules!

In addition to the black blobs, you will see on some chord boxes, white blobs. These are alternative fingerings I have included for some chords which you may find easier or more suitable for the song you are playing.

If you are reading this on an ereader, many devices such as the Kindle I suggest you find the section that relates to you (in other words, you are either Left Handed or you are not!), and then bookmark it for easy reference. If you can't jump between the chapters, just page turn to the beginning of where you want to be and bookmark that. If it's a paperback, try a good old-fashioned real bookmark! Please pay attention to the chord titles, as I don't want you struggling thinking you are playing standard right hand ukulele chords, but you are fingering left hand Baritone chords!

Finally, a list of some of the codes I have used in the chord box titles in case they were not obvious

m = minor

maj = major

b = flat

= sharp

aug = augmented chord

dim = diminished chord

LH = left handed version of chord

Bari = Baritone ukulele version of chord

LHB = Left handed baritone version of chord

I certainly hope you find the book helpful and carry it with you wherever you go.

As always, keep strumming!

Baz

STANDARD UKULELE CHORDS (GCEA)

A CHORDS

A
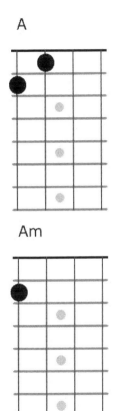

A7
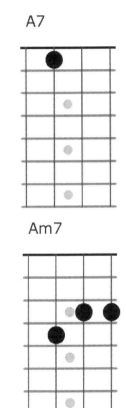

Am

Am7

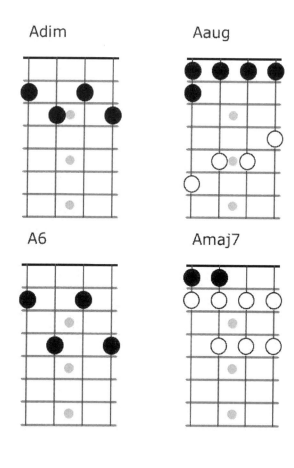

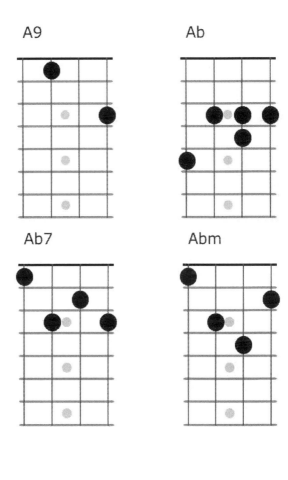

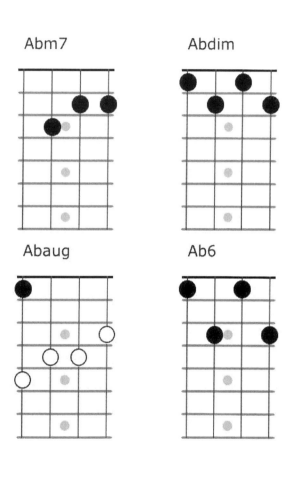

Abmaj7

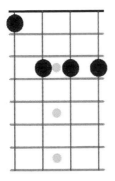

Ab9

Am6

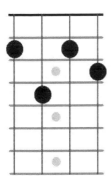

B CHORDS

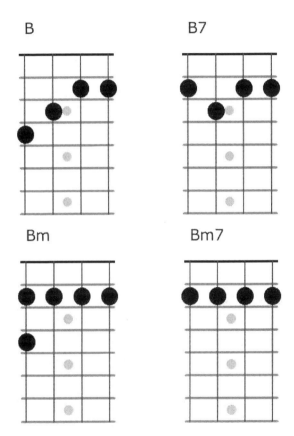

Bdim

Baug

B6

Bmaj7

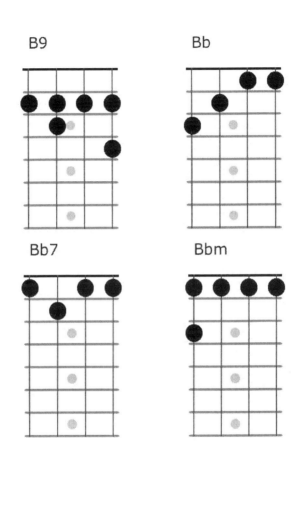

Bbm7

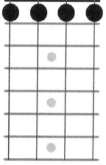

Bbdim

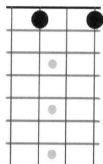

Bbaug

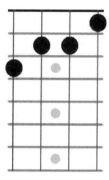

Bb6

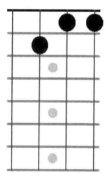

Bbmaj7

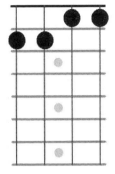

Bb9

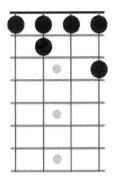

Bm6

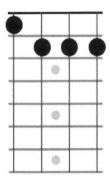

C CHORDS

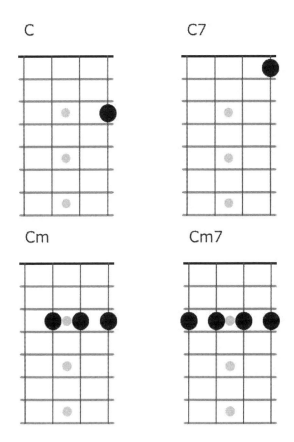

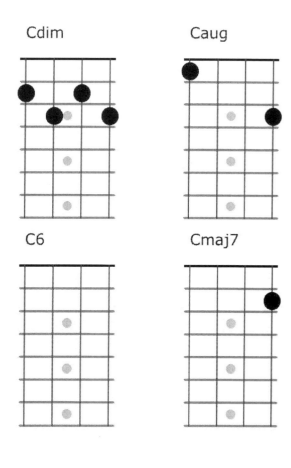

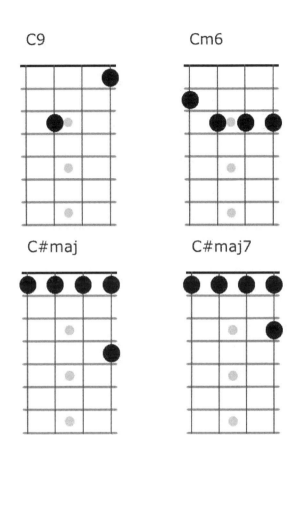

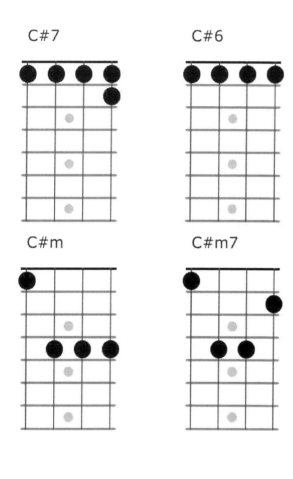

D CHORDS

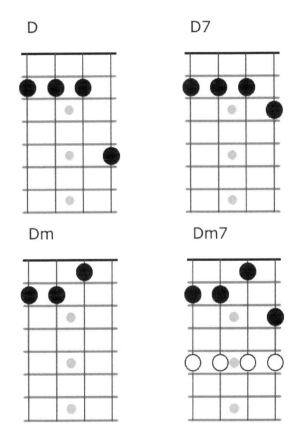

Ddim

Daug

D6

Dmaj7

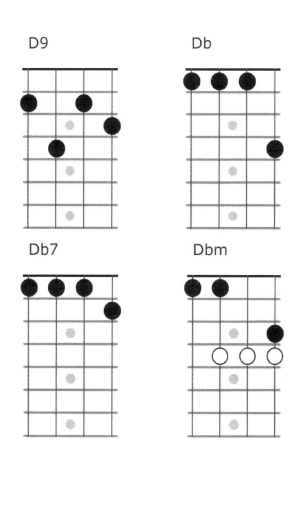

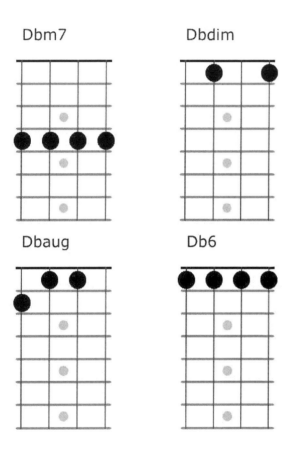

Dbmaj7

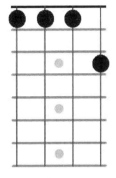

Db9

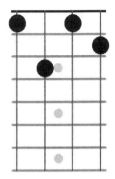

Dm6

E CHORDS

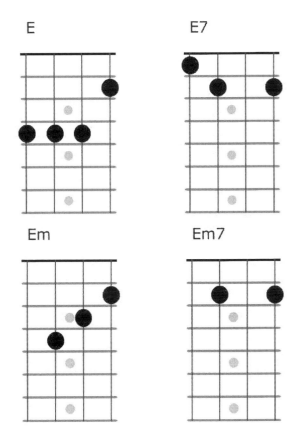

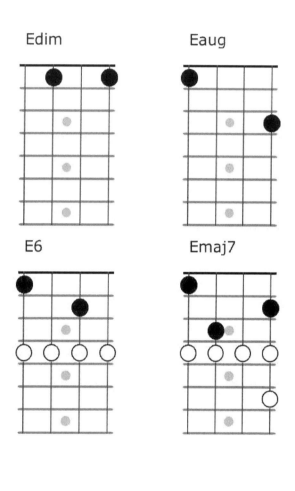

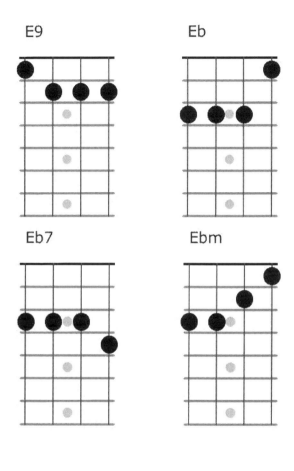

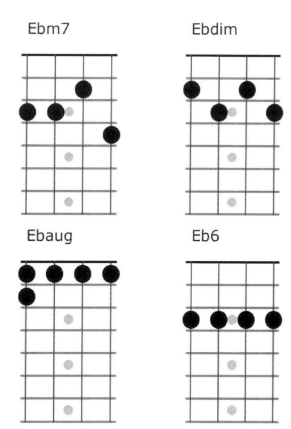

Ebmaj7

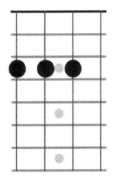

Eb9

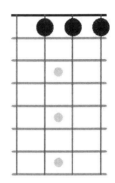

Em6

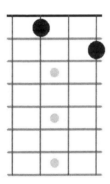

F CHORDS

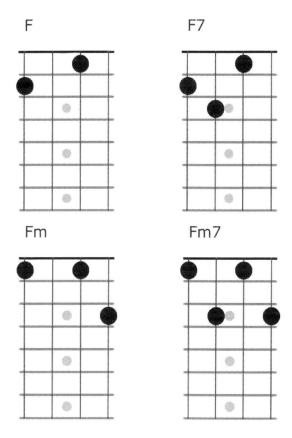

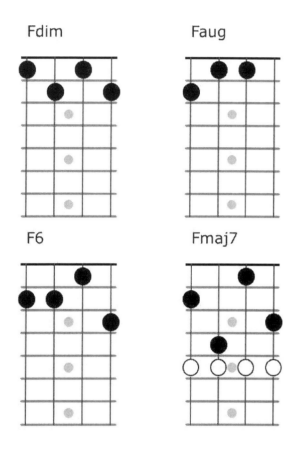

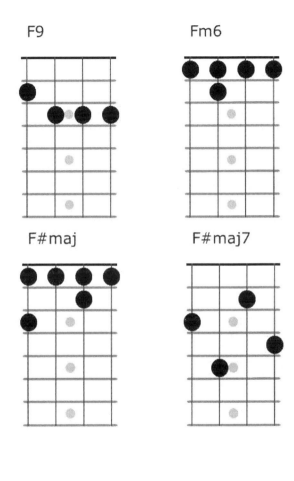

F#7

F#6

F#m

F#m7

G CHORDS

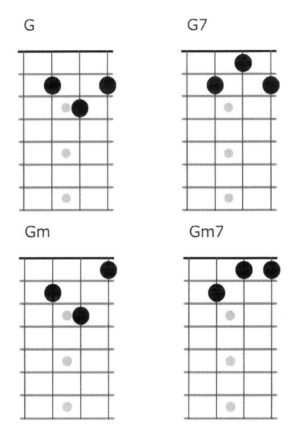

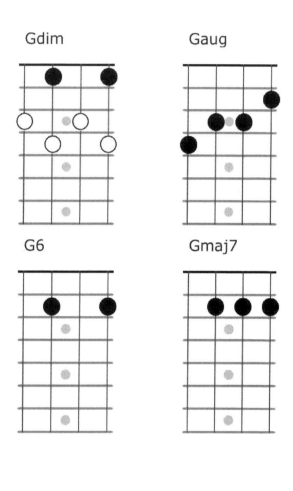

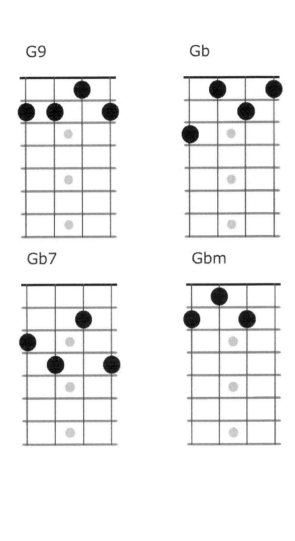

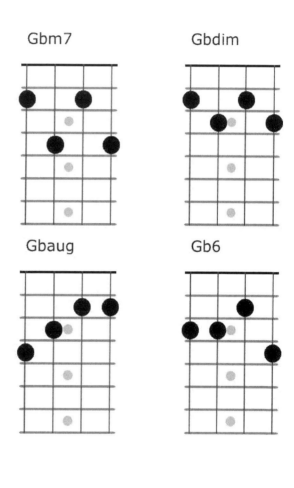

Gbmaj7

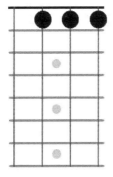

Gb9

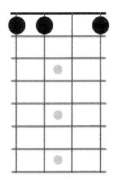

Gm6

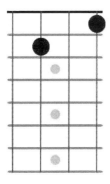

1. **STANDARD UKULELE CHORDS - GCEA (LEFT HANDED)**

A CHORDS (LEFT HANDED)

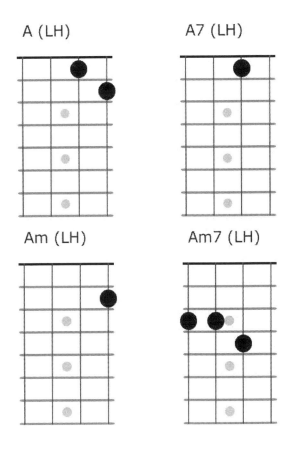

A (LH)

A7 (LH)

Am (LH)

Am7 (LH)

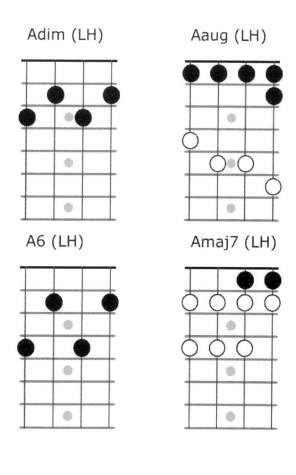

Adim (LH)

Aaug (LH)

A6 (LH)

Amaj7 (LH)

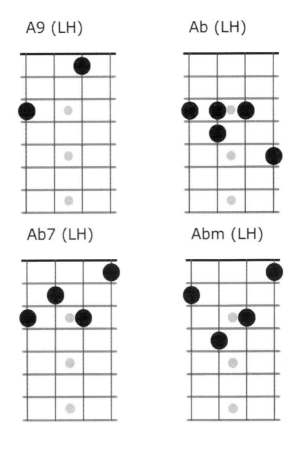

A9 (LH) Ab (LH)

Ab7 (LH) Abm (LH)

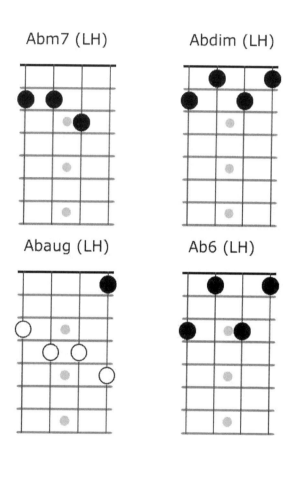

Abm7 (LH) Abdim (LH)

Abaug (LH) Ab6 (LH)

Abmaj7 (LH)

Ab9 (LH)

Am6 (LH)

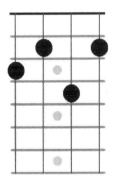

B CHORDS (LEFT HANDED)

B (LH)

B7 (LH)

Bm (LH)

Bm7 (LH)

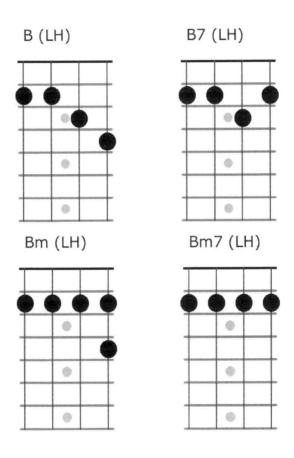

Bdim (LH)

Baug (LH)

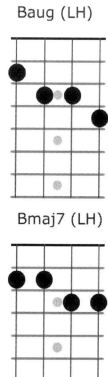

B6 (LH)

Bmaj7 (LH)

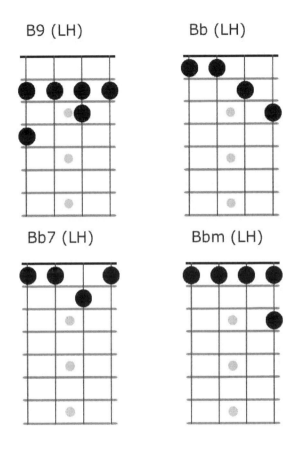

Bbm7 (LH)

Bbdim (LH)

Bbaug (LH)

Bb6 (LH)

Bbmaj7 (LH)

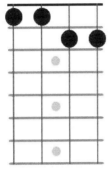

Bb9 (LH)

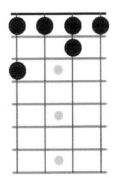

Bm6 (LH)

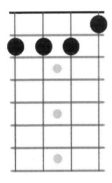

C CHORDS (LEFT HANDED)

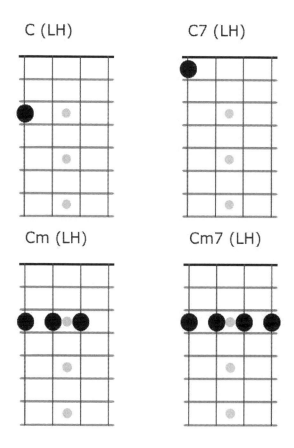

C (LH)

C7 (LH)

Cm (LH)

Cm7 (LH)

Cdim (LH)   Caug (LH)

C6 (LH)   Cmaj7 (LH)

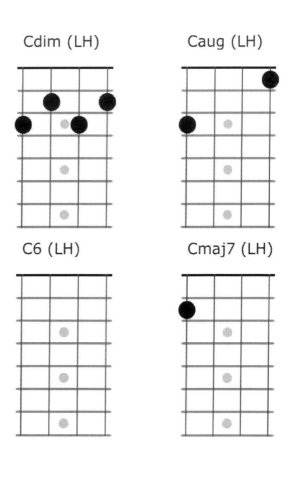

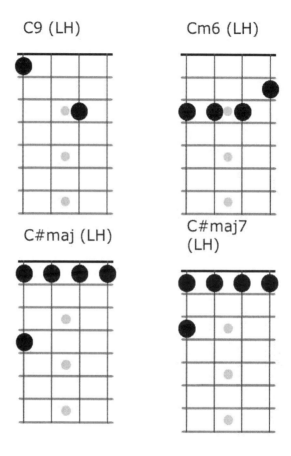

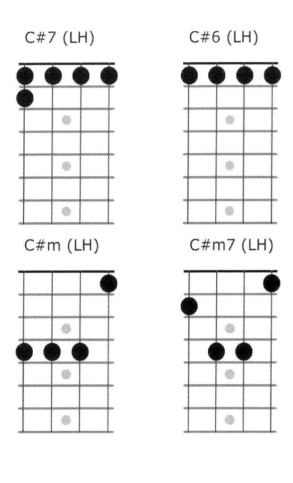

D CHORDS (LEFT HANDED)

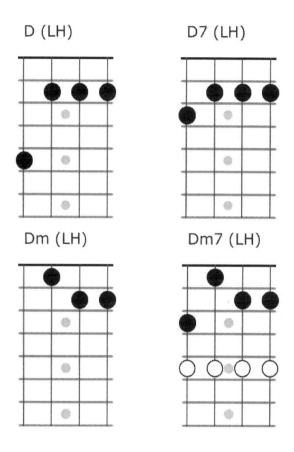

D (LH)

D7 (LH)

Dm (LH)

Dm7 (LH)

Ddim (LH)

Daug (LH)

D6 (LH)

Dmaj7 (LH)

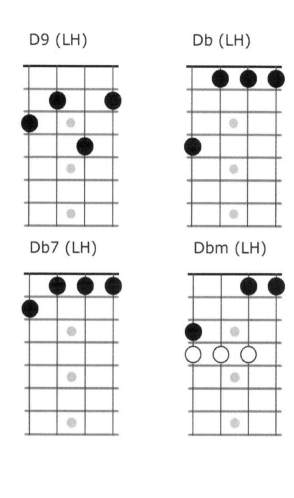

D9 (LH)

Db (LH)

Db7 (LH)

Dbm (LH)

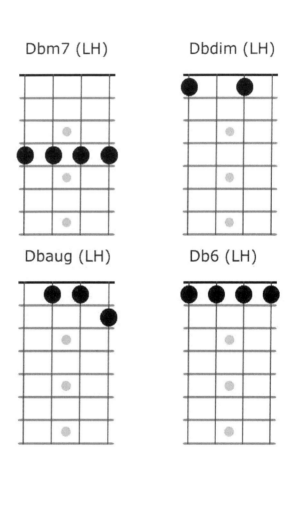

Dbmaj7 (LH)

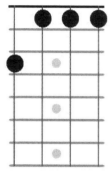

Db9 (LH)

Dm6 (LH)

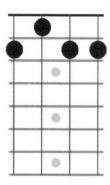

E CHORDS (LEFT HANDED)

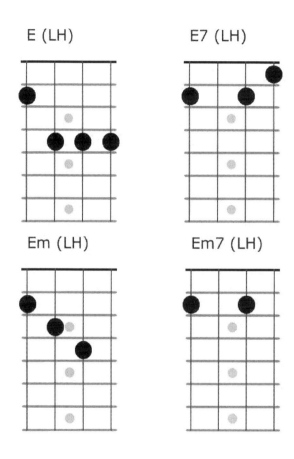

E (LH)

E7 (LH)

Em (LH)

Em7 (LH)

Edim (LH)

Eaug (LH)

E6 (LH)

Emaj7 (LH)

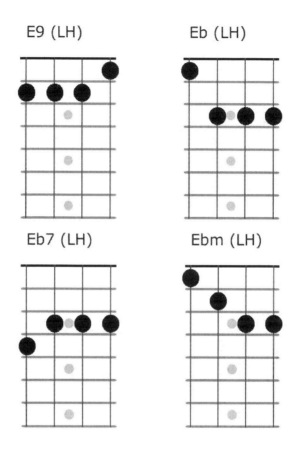

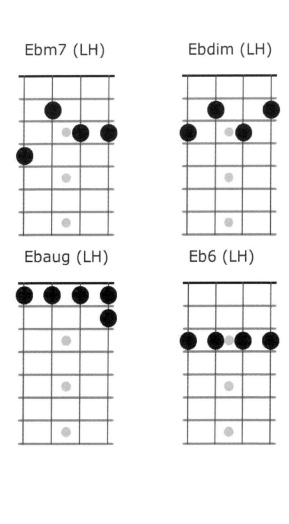

Ebm7 (LH)   Ebdim (LH)

Ebaug (LH)   Eb6 (LH)

Ebmaj7 (LH)

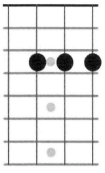

Eb9 (LH)

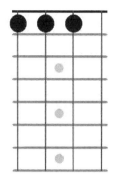

Em6 (LH)

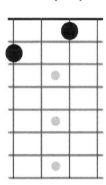

F CHORDS (LEFT HANDED)

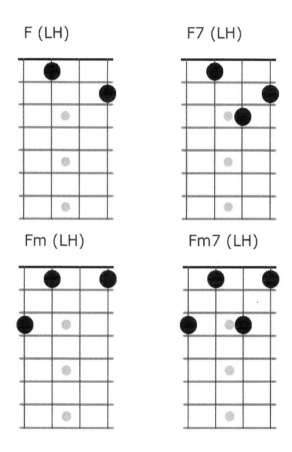

F (LH)

F7 (LH)

Fm (LH)

Fm7 (LH)

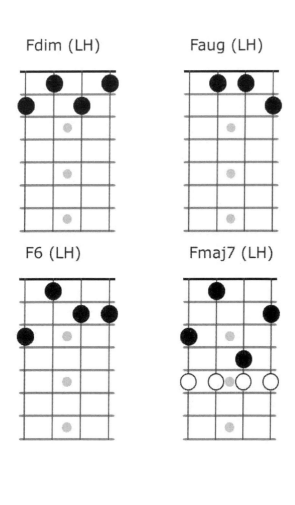

F9 (LH)

Fm6 (LH)

F#maj (LH)

F#maj7
(LH)

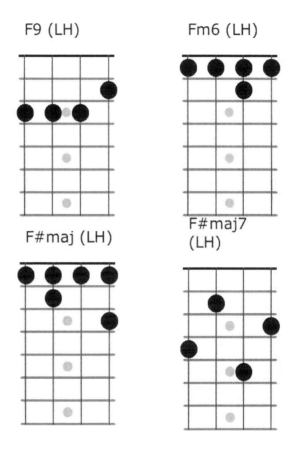

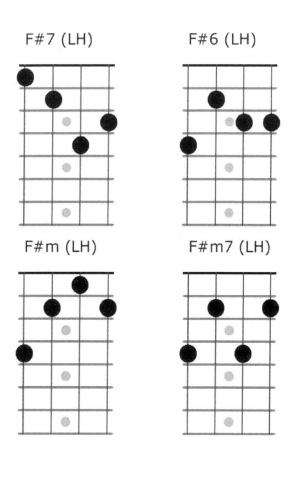

G CHORDS (LEFT HANDED)

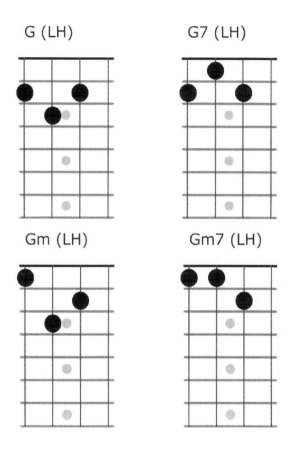

G (LH)

G7 (LH)

Gm (LH)

Gm7 (LH)

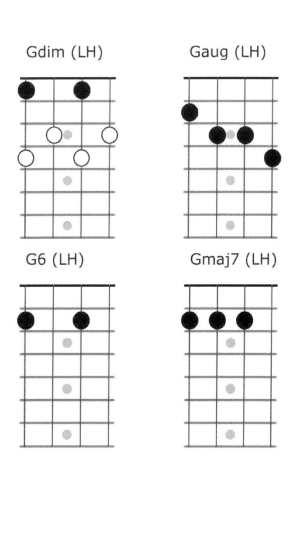

Gdim (LH)   Gaug (LH)

G6 (LH)   Gmaj7 (LH)

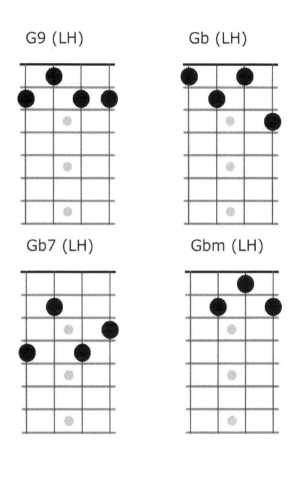

Gbm7 (LH)

Gbdim (LH)

Gbaug (LH)

Gb6 (LH)

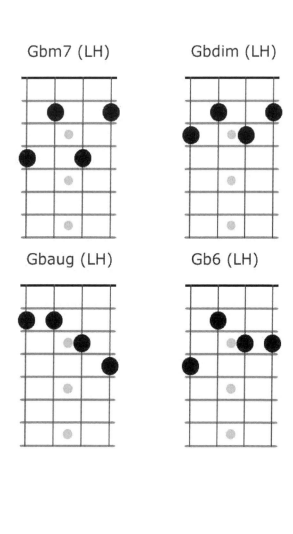

Gbmaj7 (LH)

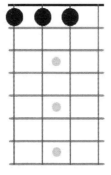

Gb9 (LH)

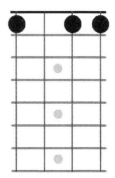

Gm6 (LH)

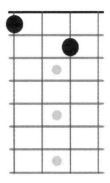

2. BARITONE CHORDS (DGBE)

A CHORDS (BARITONE)

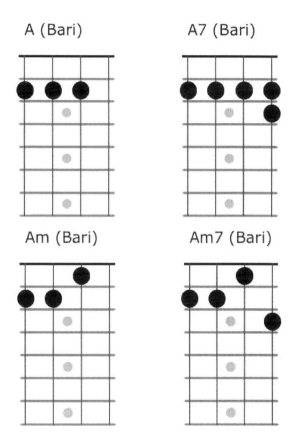

Adim (Bari)

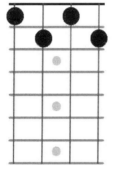

A6 (Bari)

B CHORDS (BARITONE)

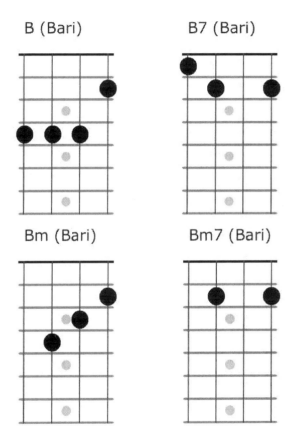

B (Bari)

B7 (Bari)

Bm (Bari)

Bm7 (Bari)

Bdim (Bari)

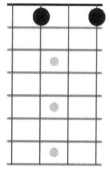

B6 (Bari)

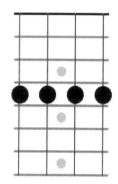

C CHORDS (BARITONE)

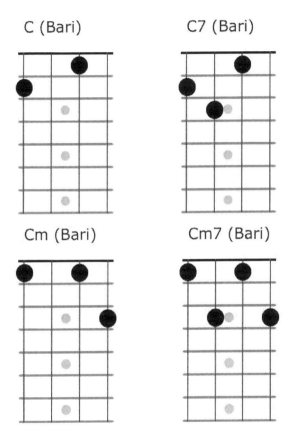

C (Bari)

C7 (Bari)

Cm (Bari)

Cm7 (Bari)

Cdim (Bari)

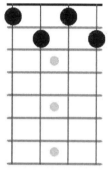

C6 (Bari)

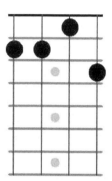

D CHORDS (BARITONE)

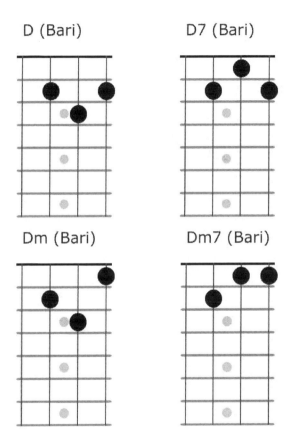

D (Bari)

D7 (Bari)

Dm (Bari)

Dm7 (Bari)

Ddim (Bari)

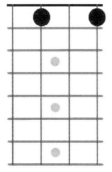

D6 (Bari)

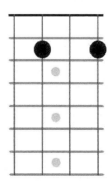

E CHORDS (BARITONE)

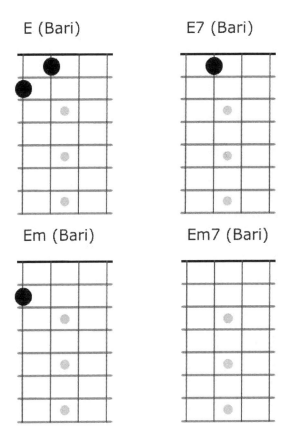

E (Bari)

E7 (Bari)

Em (Bari)

Em7 (Bari)

Edim (Bari)

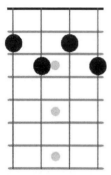

E6 (Bari)

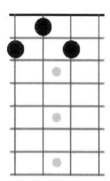

F CHORDS (BARITONE)

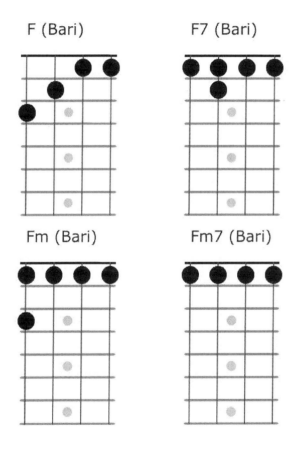

F (Bari)

F7 (Bari)

Fm (Bari)

Fm7 (Bari)

Fdim (Bari)

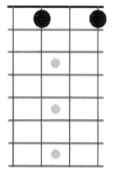

F6 (Bari)

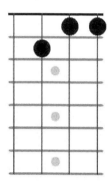

G CHORDS (BARITONE)

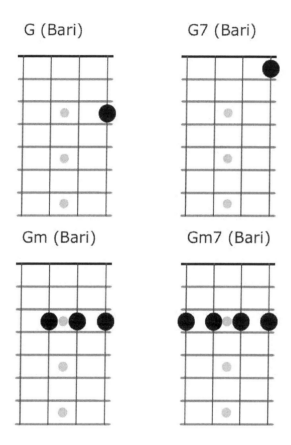

G (Bari)

G7 (Bari)

Gm (Bari)

Gm7 (Bari)

Gdim (Bari)

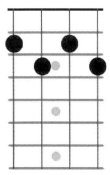

G6 (Bari)

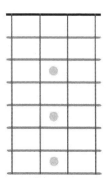

3. **BARITONE CHORDS (DGBE) – LEFT HANDED**

A CHORDS (BARITONE, LEFT HANDED)

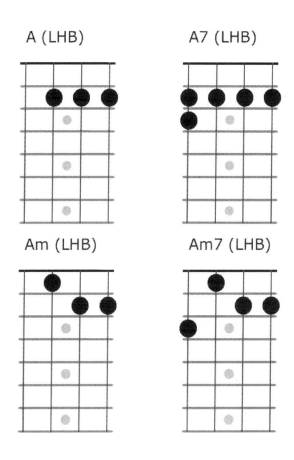

Adim (LHB)

A6 (LHB)

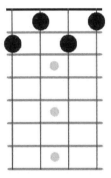

B CHORDS (BARITONE – LEFT HANDED)

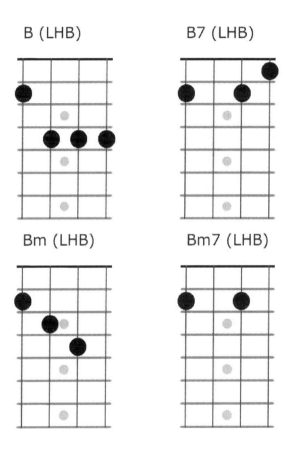

B (LHB)   B7 (LHB)

Bm (LHB)   Bm7 (LHB)

Bdim (LHB)

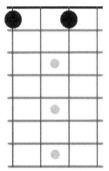

B6 (LHB)

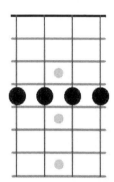

C CHORDS (BARITONE – LEFT HANDED)

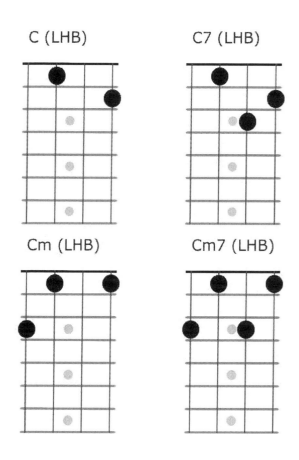

C (LHB)

C7 (LHB)

Cm (LHB)

Cm7 (LHB)

Cdim (LHB)   C6 (LHB)

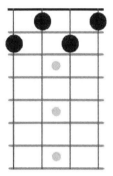 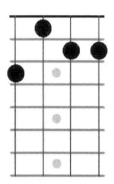

D CHORDS (BARITONE – LEFT HANDED)

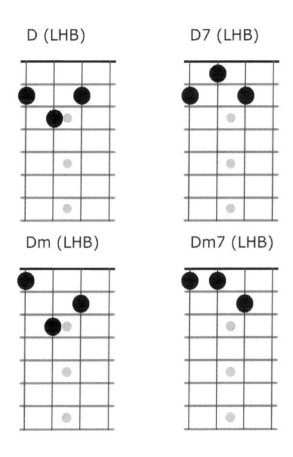

D (LHB)

D7 (LHB)

Dm (LHB)

Dm7 (LHB)

Ddim (LHB)

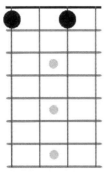

D6 (LHB)

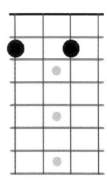

E CHORDS (BARITONE – LEFT HANDED)

E (LHB)

E7 (LHB)

Em (LHB)

Em7 (LHB)

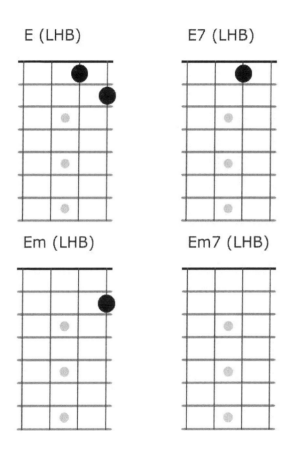

Edim (LHB)

E6 (LHB)

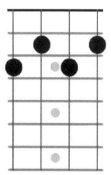 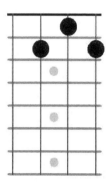

F CHORDS (BARITONE – LEFT HANDED)

F (LHB)   F7 (LHB)

Fm (LHB)   Fm7 (LHB)

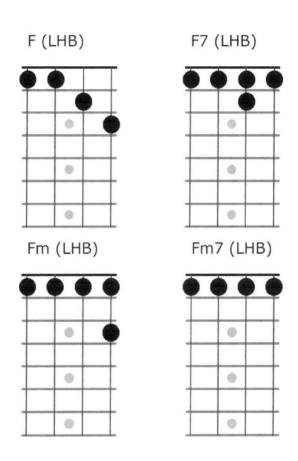

Fdim (LHB)   F6 (LHB)

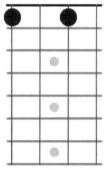 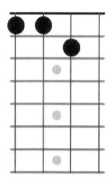

G CHORDS (BARITONE – LEFT HANDED)

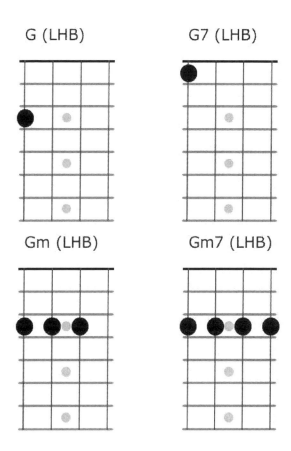

G (LHB)   G7 (LHB)

Gm (LHB)   Gm7 (LHB)

Gdim (LHB)

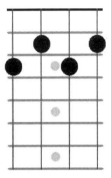

G6 (LHB)

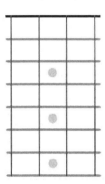

ALSO BY THE AUTHOR

What Ukulele Players Really Want To Know –
the original bestselling ukulele handbook for
beginners

More Of What Ukulele Players Really Want To
Know – the follow up!

15696727R00065

Made in the USA
Lexington, KY
11 June 2012